FOREWORD
by Ernest "Tre" Hadrick III (Mr. Lit)

In our industrialized society, written words
are a key part of people's lives. Learning to read
these words is arguably the single most
important skill that a child needs to learn.
When a child can read, they have a lifetime
of possibilities opened up to them.

Schools are working hard to meet the challenge
of teaching children to read, with a renewed
focus on teaching phonics. At the same time,
many parents often feel that they are not
equipped with the tools to help their
children learn to read and spell.

This book, aimed at helping parents, is the guide
that every parent needs to help them understand
the process of learning to read and spell.
Written by an international specialist in literacy
who cares passionately about helping all children
learn to read, this guide will take you
through everything you need to know about
how reading and spelling are taught using
phonics and how you can help at home.

My hope is that this book will go a long way in
helping you raise your own happy, confident,
and successful reading child. Be Lit!

*Tre Hadrick, also known as Mr. Lit, is an educator,
certified counselor, and community leader in
Norristown, PA. For more than fifteen years,
he has worked to advance the lives of young
children, teens, and their families. He currently
serves as a school counselor at Central Montco
Technical High School and an adjunct professor
at Villanova University. He was recently appointed
to the Pennsylvania State Board of Education.*

DK | Penguin Random House

Author Ann Sullivan

Senior Designer Louise Brigenshaw

Publisher Sarah Forbes
Managing Editor Katherine Neep
Managing Art Editor Sarah Corcoran
Project Editor Sophie Adam
Editor Hattie Hansford
Proofreader Heather Wilcox
Indexer Elizabeth Wise
Picture Researcher Samrajkumar. S
Production Editor Shanker Prasad
Production Controller Isabell Schart
DTP Designer Rohit Singh

Previously published in 2022
This edition published in the United States by DK Publishing,
a division of Penguin Random House LLC
1745 Broadway, 20th Floor, New York, NY 10019

The publisher would like to thank the following for their kind
permission to reproduce their photographs: **Depositphotos Inc:**
Rawpixel 6; **Dreamstime.com:** Yuri Arcurs 15, Monkey Business
Images 46; **Getty Images / iStock:** Liudmila Chernetska 41, E+ /
FatCamera 24, E+ / Fly View Productions 32 33, E+ / LumiNola 9.
All other images © Dorling Kindersley Limited

A catalog record for this book
is available from the Library of Congress.
ISBN 978-0-5939-5876-6

DK books are available at special discounts when purchased
in bulk for sales promotions, premiums, fundraising,
or educational use.
For details, contact: DK Publishing Special Markets,
1745 Broadway, 20th Floor, New York, NY 10019
SpecialSales@dk.com

Printed and bound in China

www.dk.com

MIX
Paper | Supporting
responsible forestry
FSC™ C018179

This book was made with Forest
Stewardship Council™ certified
paper—one small step in DK's
commitment to a sustainable future.
Learn more at **www.dk.com/uk/
information/sustainability**

Dedicated to
Diane McGuinness

With thanks to Geoff
Vaughan for his support
with the US version

A PARENT'S GUIDE TO
Phonics

Understanding How to Help your Child with Reading and Spelling

Ann Sullivan

DK Learning

CONTENTS

INTRODUCTION

Reading is one of the most important things we can teach our children. Think about all the activities involving reading that we want our children to be able to do:

- **read stories, poems, and magazines for pleasure**
- **find out information and facts from books and the internet**
- **read text in games and online activities**
- **read text in the world around them on signs and displays**

As they get older and become young adults, we want them to be able to:

- **read the news**
- **read about other people's thoughts and opinions**
- **read letters and emails**
- **read forms and official documents**
- **keep in touch with friends and family on social media**
- **continue to read for pleasure and to follow their own interests**

But there is another aspect to learning to read that is not as immediately obvious as these. As a child moves through education, they learn a wider range of subjects to a greater depth. Learning becomes more specialized, requiring them to find out information about a subject from teachers' presentations on the board, textbooks, online, and other sources.

By the time they reach grade 5, children are expected to read and write with increasing accuracy and fluency about different subjects. Accuracy means making few mistakes, and fluency means reading or writing smoothly, at a good speed, and without hesitating or repeating themselves.

So, reading and writing are the tools children need to access the school curriculum. **It is important that we set our children up to take advantage of all learning opportunities, so they can make progress and reach their potential.** Being able to confidently read and write impacts a child's long-term future.

Most people can't remember how or when they learned to read. At best, we have a vague memory of when we suddenly became able to look at words and read them like we do, almost instantaneously.

"THE AIM OF THIS BOOK IS TO DEMYSTIFY PHONICS, MAKING IT EASY TO UNDERSTAND, AND TO GIVE YOU TIPS ON HOW BEST TO SUPPORT YOUR CHILD ON THEIR JOURNEY TO BECOMING A FLUENT READER, SPELLER, AND WRITER.

Over the past 50 years, teachers have used lots of approaches to teach children to read, some more successful than others. Thanks to research, known as the **Science of Reading**, carried out at universities by academics and the work of teachers and practitioners, we can confidently say the best way to teach reading is **structured literacy with a strong emphasis on systematic phonics.** This approach to teaching reading and spelling is common in English-speaking countries.

As a parent, you may have heard the term "balanced literacy," which is the way that schools have been teaching reading up to this point. However, many are moving away from this approach in favor of structured literacy and systematic phonics because there is such strong evidence from the research that this is the most effective way to teach reading and spelling. In fact, many states have now introduced legislation mandating that districts and schools teach reading using structured literacy programs, and teachers and teaching assistants are being retrained to teach these.

Phonics can feel bewildering to parents and other adults supporting a child with their reading. After all, once we can read, it's not something we think about every day, if at all!

The aim of this book is to demystify phonics, making it easy to understand, and to give you tips on how best to support your child on their journey to becoming a fluent reader, speller, and writer.

Let's take a closer look at written language and phonics and help you support your child's reading progress today.

WHAT IS PHONICS?

Phonics is the name given to the way the foundations of reading and spelling are best taught.

It surprises many people to know that phonics is not a method of teaching. **Phonics is knowledge about how written language is put together and a set of skills that allow us to use that knowledge to read and spell words.**

Phonics teaches the link between the words we say (or think) and the words we write on the page. It teaches how the letters in written words represent the speech sounds we say in spoken words.

For example, say the word *"cat"* out loud to yourself.

When we say that word, we say quite a few sounds, but we say them in rapid succession. We hardly notice the different sounds when we speak so we need to listen carefully and take time to think about them.

Can you hear what sounds you say? You say the sounds:

$$/c/ \ /a/ \ /t/$$

If we want to write the word, we represent each of these sounds by a symbol, which we call a letter.

We write down the sounds using the letters:

$$cat$$

Basically, that's phonics!

There are just a few extra things that we need to know about, though.

Before we look at these, let's think a little more about sounds and letters.

The technical word for the **speech sounds** in spoken words is **phonemes**.

We write sounds or phonemes in forward slashes so it's clear we are talking about a sound and not a letter. For example, we write **/s/** when we talk about the first sound in the word "sit."

The technical word for the **letters** that represent the sounds is **graphemes**.

Some phonics programs teach students to use the technical terms "phoneme" and "grapheme;" others just call them "sounds" and "spellings" or "sound-spellings."

Find out which terms your child's school uses to talk about sounds and letters and use those with your child. It's good to be consistent.

→

SOUNDS AND LETTERS

PHONEME = sound

GRAPHEME = letter

= group of letters

= "sound-spellings"

= "spelling"

Now let's take a closer look at phonics.

So far, we know that when we write a word, we write a grapheme to represent each sound in it.

Writing is like a **code** children need to crack and know how to use to read and spell. Children can't crack the code themselves. They need to be taught. This is what happens in phonics lessons. It's why reading is sometimes described as **de**coding.

When we speak in English, we use about 44 different sounds in different combinations to make up and say all the many thousands of words in English.

It makes sense then, that in their phonics lessons children gradually learn about the sounds and their matching graphemes. They learn to "crack the code." Schools follow a program of study, but there are lots of different phonics programs, so find out which one your child's school uses and get to know a little more about it.

Working through any phonics program takes time, up to three years, or longer for children with special educational needs, so be patient and trust the process.

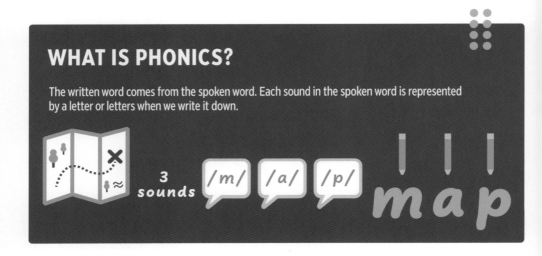

WHAT IS PHONICS?

The written word comes from the spoken word. Each sound in the spoken word is represented by a letter or letters when we write it down.

3 sounds /m/ /a/ /p/ **map**

"

WRITING IS LIKE
A CODE CHILDREN
NEED TO CRACK
AND KNOW HOW TO
USE TO READ AND
SPELL. CHILDREN
CAN'T CRACK THE
CODE THEMSELVES.
THEY NEED TO
BE TAUGHT.

SOUNDS OF
THE ALPHABET

When we start teaching a child to read, we begin by keeping things simple. We teach some basic sounds and their matching graphemes, as in the word *cat*. This gives children the opportunity to learn and understand that written language is a code, to learn and practice the key skill of blending (more about that later), and to build confidence in their reading.

Wouldn't it be great if we just had to learn one single letter for each of the sounds?

Unfortunately, English is one of the most complicated languages to learn! Here's why:

Some graphemes have more than one letter.

Have a look at these words and notice the letters in red.

*sh*op *th*in *si*ng

The sounds /sh/, /th/, and /ng/ are represented by graphemes that are made up of two letters.

It's useful at this point to know that the graphemes themselves have been given their own names depending on how many letters are in them. Your child may or may not be taught these names, depending on which phonics program is used, so check with the school. Graphemes such as *sh*, *th*, and *ng* have two letters and are called **digraphs**.

Now have a look at these words:

*ligh*t w*eigh*t

The sounds /ie/ and /ai/ are represented by graphemes that are made up of three and four letters.

> **Graphemes that have three letters are called trigraphs.**
>
> **Graphemes that have four letters are called tetragraphs.**

But there is more to think about...

Some sounds are represented by not just one but lots of different graphemes.

Let's look at some words and break this down. These all have an /oa/ sound, represented by the graphemes in red.

n*o* c*oa*t sn*ow*
t*oe* th*ough* c*o*de

As you can see, there are six ways to represent the sound /oa/ in words (the red letters).

Children learn about this in their phonics lessons and find out about the graphemes for all the sounds of the alphabet. Some people refer to this as learning the "alphabetic code."

But there's more...

Some graphemes represent more than one sound.

Look at these words that all contain the grapheme **OW**, but think about what sounds it represents in the different words.

brown   slow

In "brown" we say the **/ou/** sound but in "slow" we say the **/oa/** sound.

These complications are why it takes so long to learn the alphabetic code and why many children find it difficult, especially at first. It's also why schools use structured phonics programs that gradually teach children all about the code, working through the sounds one by one.

Have a look at the sound charts at the end of the book, which show you how all the sounds are represented by their graphemes.

Don't panic! It may all seem a little overwhelming, but remember your child will be working through this gradually at school and will bring reading books and activities home that match what they are doing in lessons—you will work alongside your child and will be able to help and support them.

BLENDING

As well as learning how to crack the code, children also need to know how to *use* it to *read* words.

When we read a word, we look at each grapheme and match a sound to it. We combine the sounds or "push the sounds together" to make the word. This is called **blending**.

Blending is a skill that children need to be taught and given the opportunity to practice. Being good at blending takes time and lots of practice and experience.

There are two ways that blending is taught in schools.

First, we can teach children to work through the word left to right, looking at each grapheme and saying the matching sound. Then, once they have done that, they go back, think about the sounds again, and "push them together" to get the word.

sit   /s/   /i/   /t/   = "sit"

Second, we can teach children to work through the word left to right, looking at each grapheme and saying the matching sound, but pushing them together as they move through the word. In this strategy, they say the first sound and keep saying it until they're ready to say the next, then say that. They keep saying that sound until they're ready to say the next, then say it ... and so on.

sit / s /   / i /   / t /   ))) = "sit"

For the word "sit," it would sound something like this "ssiit." In this way, the child just listens to the word forming and says what they hear.

You may have noticed that some sounds are easier to blend than others.

Sounds like **/ f /**, **/ l /**, **/ m /**, **/ n /**, **/ r /**, **/ s /**, **/ v /**, and **/ z /** are easy to blend, as they can be "spoken" for a few seconds. When children are first learning to blend, this is great because it gives them a tiny bit more time to think about what comes next and do what they need to do.

Sounds like **/ b /**, **/ c /**, **/ d /**, **/ g /**, **/ j /**, **/ p /**, and **/ t /** are tricky because we can't "speak" them for very long without accidentally adding an unintentional "uh" sound. So, when reading, the child must move on quickly from these sounds to the next to avoid that happening. For example, when reading the word "bed" the child must move quickly from the **/ b /** to the **/ e /** to avoid saying "bu-e-d."

It is important that children learn to say the sounds as clearly and precisely as they can to support good blending.

BLENDING AND READING

To read, children "decode" the word. Look at each grapheme, one by one, and match a sound for each.

Work through the word, from left to right, push the sounds together and say what the word is. This is called blending.

READING LONGER
WORDS

When children are first learning to read, we focus on short words to build up their confidence. After a while, we can start to introduce longer words.

Longer words are trickier simply because they have more sounds and graphemes. Longer words have so many sounds that we can't say them in one "breath." We say these words in chunks or groups of sounds, and when we speak, we can hear "the beats" within a word.

Let's look at this a little more closely.

Try saying this word out loud: *fun*

You can say all of it in one breath, one beat: *fun*

Now try saying: *funny*

Notice you say it in two beats:
fu-nny or *funn-y*

Now: *funniest*

Notice you say it in three beats:
fu-nni-est or *funn-i-est*

Chunking sounds together like this is natural to us. Each chunk of sounds within a spoken word is called a **syllable**.

Knowing this and being able to identify the beats or syllables helps us to read longer words.

There are many different accents and variations in the way we speak in different regions. Different people split words into chunks in different ways, as you can see in these examples. The important thing is to

READING LONGER WORDS

Work through the word, blend sounds into syllables, and then blend the syllables to read the word.

listen to the way *you and your child speak* and think about the way you split a word into syllables.

When we read longer words, we still use blending but in a slightly different way. Now, we are on the lookout (or listen out) for a syllable or chunk of sounds.

Let's look at this word: **finish**

The child starts out blending the sounds **/f/ > /i/ > /n/** and at this point can hear that there are enough sounds to make a good chunk or syllable "fin."

The child can set this syllable to one side and hold it in their memory. They then carry on with the rest of the word **/i/ > /sh/** and once again realize they have a comfortable chunk of sounds "ish."

Now that they have reached the end of the word, they can go back and remember the syllables they found and blend those together **"fin" > "ish"**—finish.

Having to remember syllables from earlier in the word is the reason why reading longer words is more difficult.

fantastic
⟶ ⟶ ⟶

f > a > n))) "fan"

t > a > s))) "tas"

t > i > c))) "tic"

fan > tas > tic))) "fantastic"

MOVING ON

With their new and growing knowledge of the alphabetic code and their developing skill of blending, children can "sound out" words and read them. This is the first step toward becoming a confident, accurate, and fluent reader!

But as adults, we don't sound out every word—we seem to just look at words and know them right away. This is called reading *"on sight"* or *"at a glance."* So, how does this happen? How do children move from slowly sounding out words to being able to read words as soon as they see them?

After lots of research we now understand what happens in the brain when we learn to read words on sight.

Each time a child reads a word by looking at the letters and then thinking about the matching sounds and blending, their brain learns the relationship between the sequence of sounds in the individual word and the graphemes that represent them. The sounds and graphemes are overlaid and connected in the brain for the individual word.

Over time, and with repeated practice and experience, this information is stored in long-term memory. From this point on, the information about the word can be quickly recalled when reading, and the child can read the word automatically and effortlessly, or on sight.

Lots of experience of reading (and spelling) words is needed for this process to happen, so the more practice children get, the sooner they will become fluent readers and spellers.

At the same time that the child is developing the ability to read words on sight, they are also learning about how strings of sounds relate to strings of graphemes in different words. This information is useful, as they can use it later to figure out how to read words they have never seen before.

Have a look at this word and read it:

crepuscular

Chances are that you've never seen it before, as it is an unusual word used by zoologists to describe animals that are active at twilight. Even so, you were probably able to read the word quickly by using your knowledge of phonics and of words containing similar strings of letters and sounds.

In addition being able to read words on sight, as the child learns the sounds of the alphabet and learns how to blend, their reading becomes increasingly fluent. This means that they can read accurately, with good pace (not too slow), with expression (changes of rhythm and volume that relate to the meaning of the text), and with understanding.

Our children are moving toward becoming fluent readers!

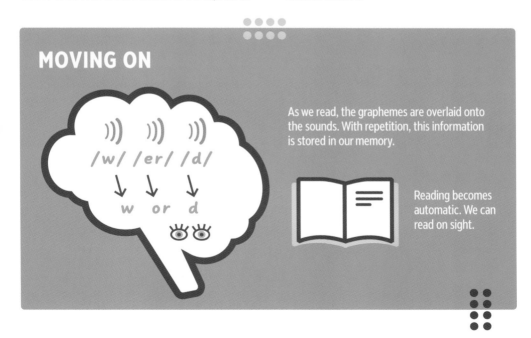

MOVING ON

/w/ /er/ /d/

w or d

As we read, the graphemes are overlaid onto the sounds. With repetition, this information is stored in our memory.

Reading becomes automatic. We can read on sight.

COMMON
WORDS

We want *all* words to become words that the child can read automatically and without effort, or on sight.

If we think about all the words we read and spell, we can see that some of them are used a lot more often than others. Words such as "the," "like," "were," and "which" pop up in text all the time. These are called "high-frequency words" or "heart words."

It would seem to make sense that if children learn these common words early, then it would give their reading a big boost. Unfortunately, many of these words have unusual graphemes in them or graphemes that are generally learned much later in a phonics program.

Let's look again at the words above. Notice the red graphemes and think about the sounds.

the like were which

We can see how these are a little more complicated than simple words, such as "**cat**."

Some programs label these common words as "tricky" or "common exception" words or even say that they "cannot be decoded," but this is not true. These words are *inconvenient*, yes, because children meet them early in their experience of learning to read before they have studied many graphemes in class. But, if we look carefully at these words, we can easily see the relationship between the sounds and their graphemes.

Let's look at an example of a common word that is said to be "tricky":

said

It has three sounds in it: **/s/ /e/ /d/**. The **s** and the **d** aren't a problem for our beginner readers, but the sound **/e/** is represented by the grapheme **ai**, which has two letters and is rare. So how do we deal with this?

Some phonics programs expect children to learn these words visually as pictures or images of the whole word (without thinking about the sounds and graphemes). This is often done by looking at flashcards of the whole word and then saying the word. Words learned this way are called "sight words."

Earlier, we talked about how children learn to read words automatically, or *on sight*, by relating the sounds to the graphemes. Now, we are using a very similar term "sight words" to mean learning words as visual whole images. These are two very different things!

We need to be mindful that our teaching follows the research on how the brain learns to read. There is a big problem with learning words as "sight words." By learning words as whole-word images, the sounds and graphemes are never overlaid in the brain. So, the child does not learn the relationship between the sounds and graphemes in the word. Because of this, the brain is not able to extract any information from the word to help read new words with similar letter patterns and strings of sounds.

COMMON WORDS

Some words are used a lot more than others:

said   great
the
friend   say

These words can be awkward for beginner readers because they contain unusual graphemes or sounds that are studied much later in a phonics program.

→

So, how do we deal with these common words early in teaching?

The key is to identify the part or parts of the word the child does not yet know and give them specific information about just that, encouraging them to then decode the word themselves by blending.

To be able to do this, it's helpful to find out the teaching order of sounds and graphemes in the school's phonics program. You will then know what your child has and hasn't studied when you work with them on their reading and spelling.

Here's an example. An early reader encounters this word in their book:

$$is$$

You know that they have worked on the sound /i/ in class, and so you can assume that they know it and can work with it. You also know that they have learned that the grapheme **S** represents the sound /s/. They have *not* yet learned that **S** can also represent the sound /z/, and it is this fact that will cause them difficulties.

So, how do you tackle this?

1 Encourage the child to start decoding the word and to begin by identifying and saying the sound /i/.

2 As they move on to the next grapheme, gently interrupt them and point to the **S** grapheme (drawing a circle around or underlining it can help the child to notice the grapheme).

3 Pointing to the **S** grapheme, say, "In this word, this is /z/, say /z/ here."

4 Support the child in starting over and blending the /i/ and /z/ sounds together.

5 The child can then blend to arrive at the word "is."

When supporting reading in this way, there is never a need to simply supply a whole word for your child. You can help them decode every word and boost their progress and confidence.

READING
WITH UNDERSTANDING

Phonics is very much about decoding. When a child uses their phonic knowledge and skills to decode text, they "lift the words from the page."

But reading is much more than that. Reading is about understanding what you have read: following the story, understanding the facts or information, or getting the message.

We could be forgiven for giving the impression that reading is just about phonics, but teachers and teaching assistants understand that phonics is the foundation, and they include lots of other important aspects of reading into their lessons and across the curriculum.

They also work on:

- **background knowledge: making sure children know about the subject of the text they are reading**
- **vocabulary: making sure children understand the meaning of the individual words they decode in the text**
- **language structure: making sure children know and understand the correct order of words in spoken sentences**

- **comprehension: making sure children learn to read between the lines as well as understand the literal meaning of the text**

In school, children work on these aspects of reading with activities often based around talking about what they have read.

When your child is reading to you, encourage them to talk about the book by asking them questions and commenting on the text yourself.

As they read, check that they know the background to the story. For example, if the story is about a wolf, they may not have seen one, know where they live, know what they eat, and so on. This is an opportunity to tell them a little more about and around the subject.

Check that your child knows what all the words mean and give a simple explanation for any unknown ones.

Discuss the story: the characters, the setting, what happens, little details on the illustrations, and ask them what they think about the book. If it is a nonfiction book, talk about what they know now and what they knew before reading.

In school, children also learn to "check themselves" as they read, spotting when they have gotten lost and need to do something to get back on track. Here are some of the things they learn to do to fix things:

1 Ask themselves, "When did I lose track?" "Where in the text did it happen?"

2 Ask themselves, "What is the problem?" "What happened?"

3 Look back over the text and ask themselves:

- "Can I read all the words?"—if not, ask for help with reading a word
- "Do I know what all the words mean?"—if not, ask for help with what a word means
- "Did I read too fast?"—if so, read it again and take more time
- "Did I lose concentration?"—if so, read it again or read it out loud if they can
- "Did I lose track of what it means?"—if so, split the text into smaller chunks and work on understanding it chunk by chunk
- "Did I stop imagining the story in my head?"—if so, read again and imagine a movie of what is happening

READING WITH UNDERSTANDING

Reading with understanding is more than just phonics.

CHILDREN NEED TO KNOW:

- the background to the story, poem, or text
- the meaning of all the words
- how we order words in sentences to make meaning
- how to read between the lines

CHOOSING
BOOKS TO READ

There is a wonderful, wide selection of books available for our young readers to look at, read, and enjoy. Whether they are interested in stories and poems or factual texts, there is something to appeal to everyone and to help develop a love of reading.

When children are first learning to read, we need to think carefully about the books we choose to share with them. It is helpful to think about what we want our children to get out of different types of books.

The books that we want children to **read out loud** to practice their reading need to be chosen carefully. We want our children to find success and enjoy the experience of reading a book themselves.

For this purpose, schools use books known as **decodable** readers that match the phonics program they are using. They are given this name because they are written to be easy for children to decode or read by using phonics. The language used in these books is right for the child's age and is chosen carefully to match the child's level of phonics knowledge and decoding skills.

Decodable books follow the phonics your child is learning in class. When reading these books, your child should be able to sound out and read most of the words. This is great for building confidence as well as practicing reading.

Decodable readers are not the only books that children should experience. Children benefit from us **reading out loud to them**. We could choose any book that might interest them: picture books, stories, poems, or factual books. The language used in these books should be right for their age, but it doesn't have to match the child's level of phonics knowledge and decoding skills

because there is no expectation that the child reads the text themselves: we do the reading for them. Children often like to look through books afterwards to look at the pictures and illustrations, and some children like to recall and retell the story as if they were reading.

Teachers and teaching assistants also choose books that are about the topic or subject the class is studying—for example "People who help us" or "The Romans." Once again, they **read out loud** to children and encourage them to ask questions and talk about what they have heard.

Decodable readers are great when children are learning to read, but there comes a point when they are no longer needed because the child has enough phonics knowledge that they can read any text appropriate for their age. Teachers and teaching assistants know when children are ready to make the move from decodables to conventional texts and will support your child in choosing the right books.

CHOOSING BOOKS TO READ

Choose books for different purposes.

TO BUILD CONFIDENCE IN READING: your child reads a decodable reader to you.

TO LISTEN TO BOOKS THAT THEY CANNOT READ THEMSELVES: you read to the child to share the story or poem.

TO LEARN ABOUT THE WORLD: select a broad range of books to read to your child.

"

BE PATIENT
AND GIVE YOUR
CHILD TIME TO
FIGURE IT OUT
BEFORE STEPPING
IN TO HELP.

HELPING
YOUR CHILD
WITH READING

It takes up to three years for children to learn the sounds of the alphabet and be able to use them to read. Children need lots and lots of practice.

So, what can you do to help and support your child at home? Here are 10 top tips:

1 Listen to your child read the books they bring home from school.

2 Encourage your child to point to the graphemes as they read. It helps them notice the relationships between the sounds and the graphemes. Pointing to graphemes will also help your child track the words and keep their place.

3 Sounding out each word can be tiring. At the start, work in short bursts of 10 minutes or so.

4 Encourage your child to say all the sounds in each word, blending them together as they go. Show them how to do it if they need a reminder. Be patient and give your child time to figure it out before stepping in to help.

5 If they get stuck on a word, figure out where exactly the difficulty is and give them the information they need. Usually, they have forgotten the sound that matches to a grapheme. Then, ask them to start again and blend through the word.

6 Support your child when they are reading a common word that contains a rare grapheme or a grapheme they haven't worked on yet.

→

7 If you notice your child is sounding out a word that you think they may know on sight, give them permission to just say it. Some children are so pleased that they can read by sounding out that they don't realize when they can read words automatically!

8 Read and reread the books your child brings home. Repeated reading of the same book is a great way to develop fluency as well as improving decoding.

9 Talk about and around the story during and after reading. Make sure that your child knows the meaning of all the words in the text, explaining any unknown ones in a very simple way. If they do not understand a sentence in the text, rephrase it so they can find the meaning.

You could talk about:

- the events of the story or the main facts of the text

- the characters: what they are like, how they might be feeling, and why they do some of the things they do

- the background to the text: for example, if the story is about putting on a play at school, talk about what a play is, about acting, about the stage, about the audience, and so on

- meanings that may be hidden in the text and show how you can read between the lines to figure out things that are not obvious right away

HELPING YOUR CHILD WITH READING

Encourage your child to:

LOOK at the word 👀

POINT to the word and track across with their finger

SPOT graphemes *b ir d*

MATCH a sound to each grapheme

BLEND the sounds together

LISTEN for the word forming)))

SAY what the word is

10 Read lots of stories to your child. These may be books you have at home or books from school or the library. These are likely to contain lots of words that your child is not yet able to read because they haven't gotten far enough into their phonics. Don't expect them to read anything—just let them enjoy sharing the story and pictures with you.

SPELLING

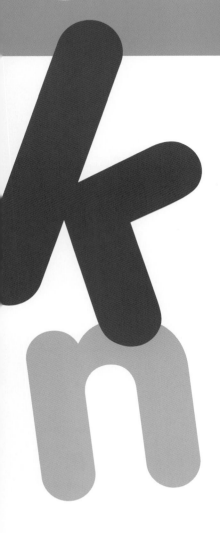

You now know that writing is a code that uses the alphabet. As well as for reading, we also use the code when we spell or write words—we just go in the opposite direction. In fact, spelling is the reverse of reading and can be described as **en**coding.

When we want to spell a word, we think about all the sounds in the word, one by one. Then we can match a grapheme to each sound, in order to write the word.

Splitting the spoken word into its sounds before spelling is called **segmenting**.

Segmenting is a skill that children need to be taught and given the opportunity to practice. Being good at segmenting takes lots of practice and experience. The more practice a child has, the better they become at knowing which grapheme to use for a particular sound in individual words.

Let's look at some examples.

Imagine a child wants to spell the word "bug." They identify the three sounds **/b/ /u/ /g/** and write three graphemes:

b u g

Imagine a child wants to spell the word "fish." They identify the three sounds **/f/ /i/ /sh/** and write three graphemes:

f i s h

Imagine a child wants to spell the word "learns." They identify the four sounds **/l/ /er/ /n/ /z/** and write four graphemes:

l ear n s

In school, your child will learn how to read and spell by using phonics. They will use their knowledge of the sounds of the alphabet and their developing skill of segmenting to spell and write words.

As well as spelling words in phonics lessons, they will also be doing more and more writing themselves. At first, these will be short sentences and simple phrases on worksheets, but soon they will be writing short stories and poems, and recording information about topics and themes.

SEGMENTING AND SPELLING

To spell, children "encode" the word.

3 sounds/ phonemes

c a sh

They think about the word they want to write and then figure out what the sounds are, one by one. This is called segmenting. For each sound, they match and write a grapheme to spell the word.

Just as for reading, when spelling longer words, it helps to think about the syllables in the word.

The child can listen to themselves saying the word and notice the beats. In this way they can split the word up into chunks of sounds or syllables. They can then work on each syllable in turn, segment it into sounds, and match the graphemes.

Let's think about this word: "perfect."

The first thing to do is to think whether the word can be split into syllables, which this word can be: "per-fect."

The child then works on each syllable, one at a time, segmenting and then matching graphemes to each sound to spell the word:

Syllable 1:	"per"	Sounds:	/p/ /er/
		Graphemes:	p er

Syllable 2:	"fect"	Sounds:	/f/ /e/ /c/ /t/
		Graphemes:	f e c t

Now they have written the word:

perfect

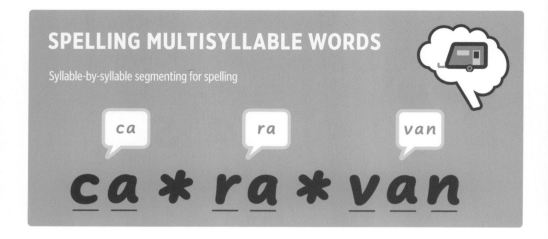

SPELLING MULTISYLLABLE WORDS

Syllable-by-syllable segmenting for spelling

ca   *ra*   *van*

ca * ra * van

HELPING
YOUR CHILD
WITH SPELLING

So, what can you do to help and support your child with spelling at home? Here are some top tips:

1 **When your child isn't sure how to spell a word, encourage them to think about the word they want to spell. Ask them to segment it to identify the sounds in it, then write a grapheme to match each sound. Finally, they can look back and check their work.**

2 **If your child brings home spellings to practice and learn, encourage them to write out the word, saying the sound at the same time as writing the matching grapheme.**

3 **Lines drawn on a whiteboard or piece of paper are helpful—one line for each sound in the word.**

f a n   l i f t

As your child learns more about the alphabetic code, they will start to spell more complex words. For example, imagine that your child wants to spell the word "dream." The word "dream" has four sounds in it so you would draw four lines on the paper.

You'd ask them to segment the word and say all the sounds in "dream": **/ d/ /r/ /ee/ /m/** .

Then ask them to say the sounds again one by one. As they say a sound, they match a grapheme and write it on the appropriate line on the whiteboard or paper, like this.

d _ _ _   d   r _ _ _

The sound **/ee/** can be represented by quite a few different graphemes, so your child will have to choose the one that is right for this word. Check out the sound charts at the end of the book. In the word "dream," the **/ee/** sound is represented by the grapheme **ea**. Your child may choose the right grapheme right away, or they may need some help.

Imagine your child thinks about the different graphemes that represent **/ee/** and chooses **ee** and completes the word.

d   r   ee _

d   r   ee m

If you think about it, they are **not wrong!** They have remembered and written a grapheme that represents the sound **/ee/**.

HELPING YOUR CHILD WITH SPELLING

Encourage your child to:

THINK about the word they want to spell

SEGMENT the word into sounds)))))))))

SAY all the sounds in the word one by one

WRITE a grapheme to match each sound *t ow n*

LOOK BACK and check their work

The point to make, though, is that **ee** is not the grapheme that we all "agree" to use. It is technically correct, but it is not the "**accepted**" spelling. Explain this to them and ask them to think of another grapheme for */ e e /*.

If your child is not sure which grapheme to write, you could write down a couple of possibilities and ask them to choose the one they think is the **accepted spelling**. If they are spelling this word before learning about the sound */ e e /* in phonics lessons, then simply write **ea** on the line for them at this stage; they will learn about this at a later point.

d   r   ea m

Familiarizing yourself with the sound charts at the end of this book will help you better support your child in this situation.

"ENCOURAGE THEM TO WRITE OUT THE WORD, SAYING THE SOUND AT THE SAME TIME AS WRITING THE MATCHING GRAPHEME.

CONCERNS
ABOUT YOUR CHILD'S PROGRESS

It usually takes around three school years to work through a phonics program, so be prepared to support your child for a good while until they become independent readers and spellers.

Learning to read and spell is one of the trickiest things that children must do, and not all children find it easy.

Some children seem to pick up reading and spelling quickly. Others may benefit from some additional teaching. Schools are aware of this, and it is increasingly common to see them providing "keep-up" sessions in addition to the class phonics lessons. When the teacher notices that a child needs a little extra practice with the sounds and graphemes being studied or needs extra practice blending or segmenting, then they direct the child to informal extra sessions to enable them to keep up. Children may dip in and out of the sessions as they need to.

Even with the keep-up sessions, some children experience a greater difficulty learning to read and spell. These children may start to lag behind other children in their class and will need additional teaching sessions to be provided on a regular and possibly longer-term basis. Schools call this type of additional teaching an intervention.

These children need to work through the phonics program at a slower pace so that they can have lots and lots of practice with sounds and graphemes. Schools need to make sure they provide phonics teaching beyond the three years usually set aside for initial instruction so that all students complete the program. With this additional option and good support to access written work in class, children should still be able to access the curriculum.

If you have any worries or concerns about your child's progress, then speak to your child's teacher sooner rather than later.

CHILDREN
WITH SPECIAL EDUCATIONAL NEEDS AND DISABILITIES

Some children may have persistent and long-term difficulties with their learning, including difficulties learning to read and spell. This may be because of underlying special educational needs and disabilities (SEND).

Children with SEND are often described as having mild, moderate, severe, or complex needs, terms that are helpful for schools and educational professionals, as they are a quick way of understanding a child's level of need in general terms.

Teachers and teaching assistants are also aware that every child is unique, and their profile of strengths and needs will be specific to them. They need to find out as much as they can about the individual child so that they can respond well and meet the child's needs in school.

Schools may call in outside professionals to carry out specialist assessments to identify a child's profile of needs and recommend what support and provision needs to be in place. Some children with SEND will be in a mainstream school, and some will be in a specialized school.

A child may have needs in one or more of these areas:

- **learning difficulties, including dyslexia**
- **autism**
- **speech**
- **language**
- **communication, including nonspeaking children**
- **sensory**
- **hearing**
- **vision**
- **physical disability**
- **social and emotional**

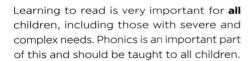

Learning to read is very important for **all** children, including those with severe and complex needs. Phonics is an important part of this and should be taught to all children.

In the US, educators are encouraged to proactively identify children with SEND at the earliest opportunity as part of a Multi-Tiered System of Supports (MTSS), a framework designed to target instruction to individual needs. It is recommended that MTSS literacy programs offer phonics teaching that considers the specific needs of every student.

Here are some examples of what this might look like:

For children with learning needs, including dyslexia, *lots and lots* of opportunities to learn about the sounds of the alphabet and practice their phonic skills should be provided. A broad range of activities at each level of a phonics program is required to maintain interest.

For children with autism, teaching should include the use of visual supports (symbols or pictures), be adapted to the length of time the child is able to focus and maintain attention on adult-led tasks, and be matched to the child's areas of interest and preferences. Incorporating sensory activities into instruction may be beneficial, while being aware of the child's sensory needs and preferences.

For children with speech and language needs, lessons should include work on spoken and written language structure, using the words and vocabulary covered in phonics lessons. Teachers and teaching assistants should work alongside the child's speech and language therapist so that therapy and teaching goals are aligned. Materials should be simple, clear, and easy to follow for children.

For children with communication needs, teaching should incorporate strategies that they use to communicate—for example, a communication board, talker, E-Tran frame, or Eyegaze system. There should also be strategies in place to allow the child to communicate what they know and what they need, such as a choice board, visual place marker, or signing.

For children with sensory needs, teaching should take place in a suitable environment, be matched to the length of time the child is able to focus and maintain attention on adult-led tasks, and be delivered regularly but "informally" rather than on a set schedule.

For children with hearing needs, the teacher and teaching assistant need to be aware of the child's hearing profile, particularly which speech sounds the child will be unable to hear even when using hearing aids. When planning phonics sessions, this should be taken into consideration, and appropriate tasks planned. For children who sign, this should be incorporated into phonics lessons.

For children with vision needs, the teacher and teaching assistant need to be aware of the child's visual profile and make adjustments as appropriate, such as enlarging text, using magnifiers, or providing extra time for tasks. When planning phonics sessions, this should be taken into consideration, and appropriate tasks set. Some children with no vision will learn Braille instead of alphabetic writing.

For children with a physical disability that affects movement of the upper body, arms, and hands, the teacher and teaching assistant should provide alternative ways to take part in activities, such as the use of tabletop cards and manipulatives, and alternative ways to record work by using a tablet with an on-screen keyboard or specialized software.

For children with social and emotional needs, the teacher and teaching assistant should be aware that they may or may not have some underlying learning needs and respond and plan accordingly. Some children may have gaps in their knowledge, and providing targeted phonics to plug those gaps will enable them to catch up and gain confidence.

Talk to your child's teacher and find out what is in place for your child and what adjustments are made so that your child can access their phonics lessons. You could apply these yourself when your child reads to you or does a phonics activity at home.

It is likely that for children with a higher level or complexity of need, it will take much longer to work through a phonics program.

This is because they need more teaching and practice with all the elements of phonics. Don't be worried if your child seems to have been learning phonics for several years.

Life with a child with severe and complex needs can be both rewarding and challenging. There are many demands on a parent or caregiver's time, and many struggle from time to time to manage it all. Don't be too hard on yourself if you can't always find the time to work with your child at home. If possible, try to set aside some time to share books and stories with them, enjoy the shared experience, and have fun together.

CHILDREN WITH SEND

LEARNING TO READ AND SPELL IS IMPORTANT FOR ALL CHILDREN.
Children with SEND need phonics teaching that considers their individual needs and is modified so that they can access all the activities.

If you have any concerns about your child's progress then speak to their teacher as soon as possible.

SUMMARY

This book gives you general information about phonics and learning to read and spell.

There are many phonics programs for schools to choose from, so it is helpful to find out which program your child's school uses and some information about it. It is particularly useful to find out the teaching order of sounds and how they teach blending. You will be able to keep track of the phonics your child will be working on in class, be prepared for the books your child brings home, and be able to help them whenever they need it.

If your child has special educational needs, find out what adjustments the school is making so that your child can access phonics. You can use the same strategies at home when your child does any reading or writing.

If you have any concerns about your child's progress, then speak to your child's class teacher as soon as possible.

Use the techniques in this book to boost confidence and support your child in their journey to become a lifelong reader!

PHONICS: A SUMMARY

You can help your child at home with their reading and spelling by thinking about phonics.

Talk about the sounds (phonemes) and letters or groups of letters (graphemes) in words.

Help them blend sounds when reading and segment words when spelling.

SOUND CHARTS

These Sound Charts can be used for reference to help you easily see how the code works.

They include:

■ A "Starting out" chart showing the sounds and graphemes your child will learn when they begin to learn to read and spell. This is sometimes referred to as basic code or initial code.

■ Three "Moving on" charts showing the sounds and graphemes your child will learn as they begin to tackle the more complicated aspects of how the code works. This is sometimes referred to as advanced code or extended code.

There are some things to bear in mind when using these charts.

They are based on generalized English pronunciation and do not account for all regional variations. Be prepared to be flexible. If a word does not fit in with the way you and your child speak, then it's fine to "move it" to another box.

The charts do not show absolutely every grapheme for the sounds but demonstrate the main ones that occur commonly. You may come across a grapheme that is not shown on the chart—for example, the *aigh* grapheme that represents the sound /ai/ in the word "straight."

SOUND CHART 1
Starting out

s **s**at	*a* **a**t	*t* **t**ap	*i* **i**n	*m* **m**at
n **n**ap	*o* **o**n	*p* **p**at	*b* **b**ag	*c* **c**ap
g **g**et	*h* **h**id	*d* **d**ad	*e* **e**lf	*f* **f**an
v **v**et	*k* **k**id	*l* **l**eg	*r* **r**ed	*u* **u**p
j **j**elly	*w* **w**ig	*z* **z**ip	*x* fo**x**	*y* **y**es

SOUND CHART 2

Moving on: sounds and their graphemes

oa	**b**oa**t**
o_e	**ho**m**e**
o	g**o**
ow	gr**ow**
oe	t**oe**
ough	th**ough**

er	h**er**
ur	b**ur**n
ir	b**ir**d
ear	l**ear**n
or	w**or**d
ar	coll**ar**

ee	s**ee**m
ea	dr**ea**m
y	happ**y**
e	b**e**
ie	f**ie**ld
e_e	**e**v**e**
i	sk**i**

oo	m**oo**n
u	tr**u**th
u_e	r**u**l**e**
ew	gr**ew**
o	d**o**
ui	s**ui**t
ou	s**ou**p
ue	bl**ue**
ough	thr**ough**

ai	tr**ai**n
a_e	m**a**d**e**
a	**a**lien
ay	pl**ay**
ea	gr**ea**t

e	r**e**d
ea	h**ea**d
a	m**a**ny

ie	**pie**
i	**mind**
y	**by**
igh	**night**
i_e	**kite**

oo	**book**
oul	**could**
u	**push**

ou	**loud**
ow	**down**
ou	**drought**

or	**for**
our	**your**
ore	**more**
oor	**door**
oar	**board**
ar	**warm**

air	**hair**
ere	**there**
are	**care**
ear	**bear**

u	**up**
o	**month**
ou	**touch**
o_e	**come**

o	**lock**
a	**want**

aw	**lawn**
a	**ball**
al	**walk**
au	**author**
ough	**bought**

ar	**star**
a	**father**
al	**calm**
ear	**heart**

oi	**soil**
oy	**boy**

i	**ink**
y	**myth**

u	**music**
u_e	**cube**
ew	**few**
ue	**cue**

ear	**near**
eer	**deer**
ere	**here**

SOUND CHART 3

Moving on: sounds and their graphemes

s	**s**at
c	**c**ity
ss	le**ss**
st	li**st**en
ce	dan**ce**
se	hou**se**
sc	**sc**ent

t	**t**op
tt	le**tt**ing
bt	dou**bt**

p	**p**et
pp	ha**pp**y

n	**n**ot
kn	**kn**ot
nn	su**nn**y
gn	**gn**at

m	**m**an
mm	su**mm**er
mn	hy**mn**
mb	la**mb**

d	**d**og
dd	la**dd**er
ed	wagg**ed**

g	**g**et
gg	wi**gg**le
gu	**gu**ard
gue	pla**gue**
gh	**gh**ost

c	**c**an
k	**k**id
ck	du**ck**
ch	**sch**ool
que	pla**que**

x	fo**x**
xc	ex**c**ept
cc	a**cc**ept

r	**r**at
wr	**wr**ong
rr	hu**rr**y
rh	**rh**ino

th	**th**in

ng	ri**ng**

z	**z**ip
s	hi**s**
zz	bu**zz**
ze	free**ze**
se	noi**se**

h	**h**at
wh	**wh**o

l	**l**amp
ll	be**ll**
le	litt**le**
el	trav**el**
il	pup**il**
al	met**al**
ol	symb**ol**

sh	**sh**ip
s	**s**ugar
s	mea**s**ure
ch	ma**ch**ine
ci	spe**ci**al
ti	poten**ti**al

b	**b**at
bb	ro**bb**er
bu	**bu**ild

j	**j**elly
g	**g**iant
ge	lar**ge**
dge	bri**dge**

f	**f**an
ph	**ph**one
ff	stu**ff**
gh	cou**gh**

ch	**ch**ips
tch	ma**tch**

v	**v**an
ve	ha**ve**

w	**w**ig
wh	**wh**ich

qu	**qu**ick

SOUND CHART 4

Moving on: focusing on graphemes

s

sun
his
sugar

ow

snow
town

u

cup
flu
music

o_e

home
move
love
gone

a

cat
baby
wasp
many
father

ea

team
great
head

oo

moon
wood

y

yes
jelly
sky
gym

i

ink
kind
ski

o

go
do
month
dog

ou

cloud
soup
touch

ough

dough
drought
through
bought

c

cat
city

ear

learn
bear
heart
near

ie

field
pie

ere

were
there
here

GLOSSARY

accepted spelling
the conventional spelling of a word that
"everyone agrees on"—a useful term to
help children when they make plausible
spelling mistakes, such as "dreem" rather
than "dream"

accuracy
correctly applying knowledge of
phonemes and graphemes and using the
key skills of blending and segmenting to
successfully read a printed or written word
or to spell a word

background knowledge
the child's general knowledge of the
subject of the book they are reading—
having good background knowledge helps
reading comprehension

balanced literacy
an approach to teaching reading that
includes "whole language" (focusing on
meaning) with minimal, unstructured
phonics input

blending
the ability to "push" different phonemes
together or combine them to make a
spoken word

choice board
a board on which 2 or 3 picture symbols
are placed with the child, and the child
then selects the symbol that corresponds
to their choice

code knowledge
what the child knows about the alphabetic
code and the phonemes and the
graphemes that represent them

communication board
a communication system used by pre-
and nonverbal children who can point to
picture symbols on a board to indicate
what they want to say

decodable reader
a reading book that matches a child's
current knowledge of the sounds of
the alphabet

decode / decoding
reading a written or printed word—a child
reads by applying their knowledge of
phoneme-grapheme correspondences
and key skills

digraph
a grapheme that is made up of two letters

encode / encoding
spelling and writing a spoken or thought word—a student spells the word by applying their knowledge of phoneme-grapheme correspondences and key skills

E-Tran frame
an Eye Transfer frame is a communication system used by pre- and nonverbal children who also have a physical disability. They look at and dwell their gaze on symbols placed around a Perspex frame to indicate what they want to say

evidence-led
guided by the results and findings of scientific, academic research

expression
the ability to read text so that it sounds like natural speech—includes intonation (change in pitch), rhythm, and stress (emphasis given to syllables and key words and phrases)

Eyegaze
the principle of a child looking at and dwelling their gaze on something to indicate that they choose it to communicate or answer questions. Used by pre- and nonverbal children who also have a physical disability

fluency
the ability to read with accuracy, automaticity, pace, and expression—the reading sounds like natural speech

grapheme
a visual form or figure that is written to represent a phoneme

language structure
the correct order of words in a sentence

letter formation
the act of writing a letter—forming a letter shape by using a pen or pencil

MTSS
stands for Multi-Tiered System of Supports, a framework many schools use to give targeted support to children with SEND

pace
the ability to read at an appropriate speed without compromising decoding accuracy or understanding

phoneme
the smallest unit of sound in a spoken word

phonics
a body of knowledge about the correspondences between phonemes and graphemes. This includes key skills—blending and segmenting—and the understanding of some simple concepts about how written language works

read a word "on sight"
the ability to look at a word and rapidly read it, apparently without any conscious effort

reading comprehension
the ability to read and understand text

Science of Reading
a general term that refers to the academic research into how children learn to read, spell, and write which provides the evidence that informs teaching practice

segmenting
the ability to split a spoken word up into its phonemes in sequence

SEND
stands for special educational needs and disabilities

sight word
a word that is learned and recalled as a visual "whole picture" without any phonic input (not to be confused with reading a word "on sight" with phonic input)

sounds of the alphabet
the way the 44 phonemes (sounds) are represented by graphemes (letter and letter combinations). This is sometimes called the "alphabetic code"

structured literacy
teaching all aspects of literacy systematically and explicitly

syllable
a group of sounds in a word that are spoken as a "beat" in natural speech

synthetic phonics
teaching the sounds of the alphabet and key skills by the synthesis or creation of

words from their smallest parts: phonemes and graphemes

systematic phonics
teaching the sounds of the alphabet and key skills in a highly structured and incremental sequence

tetragraph
a grapheme made up of four letters

trigraph
a grapheme made up of three letters

visual place marker
a simple communication system that can be used in lessons by teachers and teaching assistants with pre- or nonverbal children. When working on sounds, reading words, phrases, or sentences, the adult offers different choices, each anchored to a dot on the visual place marker. The child listens and makes their choice by pointing

vocabulary
words that a child has heard, can remember, and knows the meaning of

whole word reading
reading text by learning words as visual "whole pictures" without phonic input

word recognition
the ability to read a word either by applying phonics knowledge and skills to decode it or by reading it automatically or on sight

INDEX

→

→

ABOUT THE AUTHOR

Ann Sullivan has more than 30 years' experience
in mainstream and specialized education. Based
in the UK, her career includes roles as a literacy
teacher, a school-based Special Educational
Needs Coordinator (SENCO), an advisory teacher
for students with special educational needs, and
a Specialist Leader in Education (SLE). She has
authored multiple books on teaching phonics
to learners with special educational needs.